TEXAS TEST PREP

Practice Test Book

STAAR Math

Grade 6

ISBN 978-1466464063

CONTENTS

INTRODUCTION
For Parents, Teachers, and Tutors

About the Book

This test booklet contains three complete STAAR math grade 6 tests. The tests are just like the STAAR tests given by the state. Each test contains 52 questions, which is the same as the state test. Each test has the same question types and styles, and tests the same skills.

If the student can master the STAAR math tests in this book, they will be prepared and ready to master the STAAR state tests.

Taking the Test

Each test contains 52 multiple choice and open ended questions. Students can answer the questions by filling in the circle of their answer choice in the test booklet, or by writing their answer on the line. Students can also answer the questions by completing the answer sheet.

STAAR Math Skills

The STAAR test given by the state of Texas tests a specific set of skills and knowledge. The tests in this book cover all of the skills that grade 6 students are taught and tested on. The answer key identifies the skill tested by each question, as well as the general topic.

Use the topics and skills listed in the answer key to determine the areas of strength and weakness. Then target revision and instruction accordingly.

Score Tracker

After marking each test, record the score in the Score Tracker at the end of the book. As the student progresses through the tests, test scores will continue to improve as the student gains experience, knowledge, and confidence.

STAAR MATH

GRADE 6

TEST 1

Instructions

The test contains multiple choice and open ended questions. Read each question carefully. For multiple choice questions, select the best answer and fill in the bubble for the answer you have chosen. For open ended questions, write your answer on the line.

You can use the mathematics charts on the next two pages to help you with some of the questions.

MATHEMATICS CHART

You may use this chart to help you answer questions in the test.

LENGTH

Metric	Customary
1 kilometer = 1000 meters	1 mile = 1760 yards
1 meter = 100 centimeters	1 mile = 5280 feet
1 centimeter = 10 millimeters	1 yard = 3 feet
	1 foot = 12 inches

CAPACITY AND VOLUME

Metric	Customary
1 liter = 1000 milliliters	1 gallon = 4 quarts
	1 gallon = 128 fluid ounces
	1 quart = 2 pints
	1 pint = 2 cups
	1 cup = 8 fluid ounces

MASS AND WEIGHT

Metric	Customary
1 kilogram = 1000 grams	1 ton = 2000 pounds
1 gram = 1000 milligrams	1 pound = 16 ounces

TIME

1 year = 365 days	1 day = 24 hours
1 year = 12 months	1 hour = 60 minutes
1 year = 52 weeks	1 minute = 60 seconds

MATHEMATICS CHART

You may use this chart to help you answer questions in the test.

Perimeter	square	$P = 4s$
	rectangle	$P = 2l + 2w$

Circumference	circle	$C = 2\pi r$ or $C = \pi d$

Area	square	$A = s^2$
	rectangle	$A = lw$ or $A = bh$
	triangle	$A = \frac{1}{2}bh$
	trapezoid	$A = \frac{1}{2}(b_1 + b_2)h$
	circle	$A = \pi r^2$

Volume	cube	$V = s^3$
	rectangular prism	$V = lwh$

Pi	π	$\pi \approx 3.14$

1   Malcolm surveyed some people to find out how many pets they owned. The line plot shows the results of the survey.

Number of Pets

	X			
X	X			
X	X			
X	X	X		
X	X	X	X	X
X	X	X	X	X
0	1	2	3	4

Which conclusion can be drawn from the line plot?

Ⓐ   Every person owned at least 1 pet.

Ⓑ   The most common number of pets owned was 2.

Ⓒ   Over half the people owned exactly 1 pet.

Ⓓ   The same number of people owned 3 pets as 4 pets.

2 A triangle has angles of 50° and 75°. What is the measure of the third angle?

    Ⓐ   25°

    Ⓑ   45°

    Ⓒ   55°

    Ⓓ   75°

3 Which of these is the best estimate of the amount of liquid the cup below can hold?

    Ⓐ   200 pints

    Ⓑ   200 gallons

    Ⓒ   200 milliliters

    Ⓓ   200 liters

4   A diner sells three sizes of orange juice. The table shows the number of orange juices of each size sold in one day.

Size	Number Sold
Small	162
Medium	257
Large	188

Which of these is the closest estimate of how many orange juices were sold in all?

Ⓐ   590

Ⓑ   600

Ⓒ   610

Ⓓ   620

5   The ratio of students to teachers on a school trip was 9 to 2. If there were 6 teachers on the school trip, how many students were there?

Ⓐ   54

Ⓑ   12

Ⓒ   66

Ⓓ   27

6 Which point best represents the location of the ordered pair $(1\frac{1}{4}, 2\frac{1}{2})$?

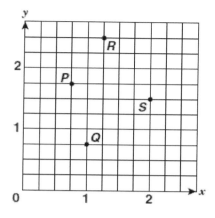

Ⓐ   Point *P*

Ⓑ   Point *Q*

Ⓒ   Point *R*

Ⓓ   Point *S*

7 A circle has a diameter of 6 inches. What is the circumference of the circle?

Ⓐ   3π inches

Ⓑ   6π inches

Ⓒ   12π inches

Ⓓ   36π inches

8   Marcus sold drinks at a lemonade stand. The table shows how many drinks of each size he sold.

Size	Number Sold
Small	15
Medium	20
Large	5
Extra large	10

Which size drink made up $\frac{3}{10}$ of the total drinks sold?

Ⓐ   Small

Ⓑ   Medium

Ⓒ   Large

Ⓓ   Extra large

9   A personal assistant can type at a speed of 85 words per minute. Which method can be used to find how many minutes it would take her to type 3,600 words?

Ⓐ   Add 85 and 3,600

Ⓑ   Subtract 85 from 3,600

Ⓒ   Multiply 3,600 by 85

Ⓓ   Divide 3,600 by 85

10   An Italian restaurant sells four types of meals. The restaurant owner made this table to show how many meals of each type were sold one night.

Meal	Number Sold
Pasta	16
Pizza	16
Salad	11
Risotto	9

What is the mean of the number of each meal sold?

Ⓐ   9

Ⓑ   13

Ⓒ   13.5

Ⓓ   16

11   A company has 28 salespersons. Each salesperson works about 37 hours each week. About how many hours do all the salespeople work in all?

Ⓐ   70

Ⓑ   600

Ⓒ   900

Ⓓ   1,200

12   What is the measure of the angle shown below?

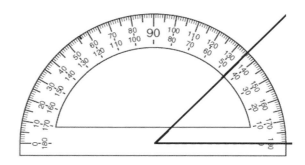

Ⓐ   45°

Ⓑ   55°

Ⓒ   135°

Ⓓ   145°

13   Which of these units would be best to use to measure the length of a box of tissues?

Ⓐ   Grams

Ⓑ   Kilograms

Ⓒ   Centimeters

Ⓓ   Meters

14   The fine for having a movie overdue is a basic fee of $5 plus an additional $2 for each day that the movie is overdue. Which equation can be used to find *c*, the cost in dollars of the fine for *d* days?

    Ⓐ $c = 2d + 5$

    Ⓑ $c = 5d + 2$

    Ⓒ $c = 2(d + 5)$

    Ⓓ $c = 5(d + 2)$

15   Yvonne needs to add the fractions below.

$$\frac{1}{5}, \frac{2}{7}, \frac{3}{10}$$

Yvonne first needs to determine the least common multiple of the denominators. Which of the following is the least common multiple of the denominators?

    Ⓐ   35

    Ⓑ   50

    Ⓒ   70

    Ⓓ   350

16 What is the rule to find the value of a term in the sequence below?

Position, n	Value of Term
1	3
2	5
3	7
4	9
5	11

Ⓐ $4n - 4$

Ⓑ $3n$

Ⓒ $2n + 1$

Ⓓ $n + 2$

17   During the baseball season, Elton's team won 5 of the 14 games it competed in.

What fraction of its games did the team win?

Ⓐ $\dfrac{5}{14}$

Ⓑ $\dfrac{14}{19}$

Ⓒ $\dfrac{5}{19}$

Ⓓ $\dfrac{5}{9}$

18 What kind of angle is angle C?

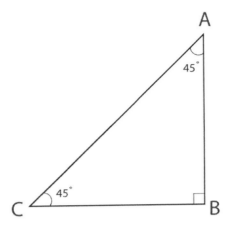

Ⓐ Acute

Ⓑ Right

Ⓒ Obtuse

Ⓓ Straight

19 Look at the expression below.

$$(16 + 20) - 8 \div 4$$

What is the value of the expression?

Write your answer on the line below.

_____

20   Which group shows all the common factors of 24 and 32?

Ⓐ   1, 2, 4

Ⓑ   1, 2, 4, 8

Ⓒ   1, 2, 4, 6, 8

Ⓓ   1, 2, 4, 8, 12

21   The ratio of boys to girls in a cooking class is 4 to 5. Which of these could be the number of boys and girls in the cooking class?

Ⓐ   12 boys, 20 girls

Ⓑ   25 boys, 20 girls

Ⓒ   16 boys, 20 girls

Ⓓ   9 boys, 15 girls

22 The table shows the number of students in each grade at Lyons Middle School.

Grade	Number of Students
Grade 6	80
Grade 7	60
Grade 8	60

Which graph best displays the data?

Students at Lyons Middle School

Students at Lyons Middle School

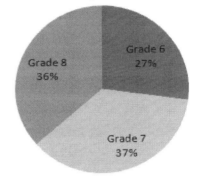

Students at Lyons Middle School

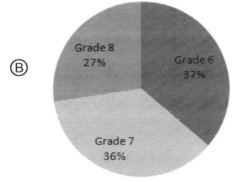

Students at Lyons Middle School

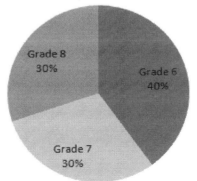

23   The drawing below shows the diameter of a circle.

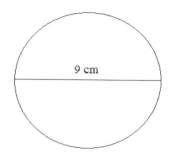

9 cm

Which expression can be used to find the circumference of the circle in centimeters?

Ⓐ   9 x π

Ⓑ   (9 x 2) x π

Ⓒ   (9 ÷ 2)^2 x π

Ⓓ   (9 ÷ 2) x π

24   Which decimal is equivalent to the fraction $\frac{5}{8}$?

Ⓐ   0.125

Ⓑ   0.375

Ⓒ   0.58

Ⓓ   0.625

25   The drawing below shows a kite.

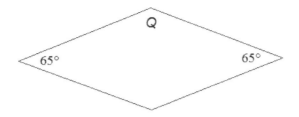

What is the measure of angle *Q*?

Ⓐ   57.5°

Ⓑ   65°

Ⓒ   115°

Ⓓ   230°

26   Juan filled a 5 liter bucket with water. What is the volume of the bucket in milliliters?

Ⓐ   500 mL

Ⓑ   5 000 mL

Ⓒ   50 000 mL

Ⓓ   500 000 mL

27 Karen made this table to show her monthly phone bills.

Month	Amount
April	$5.42
May	$5.39
June	$5.51
July	$5.27

In which month was Karen's phone bill the least?

Ⓐ   April

Ⓑ   May

Ⓒ   June

Ⓓ   July

28 A bowl contains 12 apples and 18 oranges. What is the ratio of apples to oranges?

Ⓐ   2:3

Ⓑ   3:2

Ⓒ   1:3

Ⓓ   1:2

29 The angle that is formed between two lines has a measure of 34°. Which term describes this angle?

Ⓐ   Acute

Ⓑ   Right

Ⓒ   Obtuse

Ⓓ   Straight

30 The number set below represents the number of questions that eight students answered correctly on a test.

42, 67, 87, 65, 67, 73, 86, 84

Which measure of data is represented by the number 67?

Ⓐ   Mode

Ⓑ   Median

Ⓒ   Mean

Ⓓ   Range

31 There are 40 tags in a bag. The table shows the number of tags of each color.

Color	Number
Red	12
Green	8
Yellow	16
Blue	4

Owen selects a tag at random. Which color tag has a 1 in 5 chance of being selected?

Ⓐ   Red

Ⓑ   Green

Ⓒ   Yellow

Ⓓ   Blue

32 What is the least common multiple of 3, 4, and 8?

Write your answer on the line below.

_____

33   William surveyed students on how long it took them to travel to school each morning. The table shows the results.

Time	Number of Students
0 to 10 minutes	22
11 to 30 minutes	36
31 to 60 minutes	14
Over 60 minutes	3

Which type of graph would William be best to use to summarize the survey results?

Ⓐ   Histogram

Ⓑ   Line plot

Ⓒ   Line graph

Ⓓ   Stem and leaf plot

34   The lowest temperature for June was 14 degrees below zero Celsius. What integer represents the lowest temperature for June in degrees Celsius?

Ⓐ   0

Ⓑ   14

Ⓒ   −14

Ⓓ   −28

35 Cassandra drew a pentagon on a coordinate grid, as shown below.

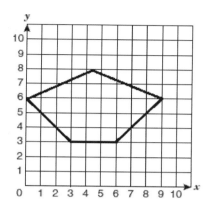

Which of these is a coordinate of one of the vertices of the pentagon?

Ⓐ   (6, 6)

Ⓑ   (9, 6)

Ⓒ   (3, 4)

Ⓓ   (5, 8)

36 Cornelia has a set of measuring cups. Which measuring cup is greater than the $\frac{1}{2}$ cup?

Ⓐ $\frac{3}{8}$ cup

Ⓑ $\frac{7}{16}$ cup

Ⓒ $\frac{1}{8}$ cup

Ⓓ $\frac{9}{16}$ cup

37 Which term describes the angle shown below?

Ⓐ Acute

Ⓑ Right

Ⓒ Obtuse

Ⓓ Straight

38   Hannah cut out a piece of fabric to use for an art project. The length of the fabric was 9.5 yards. The width of the fabric was 3.6 yards less than the length. What was the width of the fabric?

Ⓐ   5.9 yards

Ⓑ   6.9 yards

Ⓒ   12.1 yards

Ⓓ   13.1 yards

39   Which number goes in the box to make the prime factorization of 224 correct?

$$2^{\square} \cdot 7$$

Ⓐ   3

Ⓑ   4

Ⓒ   5

Ⓓ   6

40 The table below shows the total cost of hiring DVDs for different numbers of DVDs.

Number of DVDs	Total Cost
2	$6
5	$15
6	$18
8	$24

Which equation could be used to find the total cost, c, of hiring x DVDs?

Ⓐ $c = x + 4$

Ⓑ $c = 3x$

Ⓒ $c = x + 3$

Ⓓ $c = 8x$

41   The table shows the side length of a square and the area of a square.

Side Length, x (inches)	Area, y (square inches)
2	4
3	9
4	16
5	25

Which equation represents the relationship between side length and area?

Ⓐ $y = x + 2$

Ⓑ $y = 5x$

Ⓒ $y = x^2$

Ⓓ $y = 4x$

42   What is the greatest common factor of 8, 24, and 32?

Ⓐ   2

Ⓑ   4

Ⓒ   8

Ⓓ   16

43 Camille cooked a cake on high for $1\frac{1}{4}$ hours. She then cooked it for another $\frac{1}{2}$ hour on low. Which diagram represents how long she cooked the cake for in all?

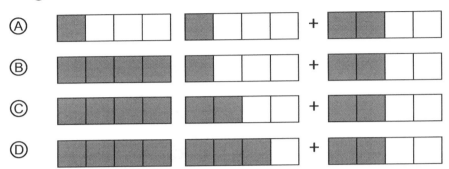

44 A piece of note paper has side lengths of 12 centimeters. What is the area of the piece of note paper?

Ⓐ   48 square centimeters

Ⓑ   72 square centimeters

Ⓒ   120 square centimeters

Ⓓ   144 square centimeters

45 Anne has 3 books. She chooses 2 books to read.

If the books are represented as A, B, C, which list represents all the possible sets of two books that Anne could choose?

Ⓐ AA, BB, CC

Ⓑ AB, BC

Ⓒ AB, AC

Ⓓ AB, AC, BC

46 Chan spent $\frac{2}{5}$ of his allowance on a gift for his sister. Which decimal represents how much of his allowance he spent?

Ⓐ 0.2

Ⓑ 0.25

Ⓒ 0.4

Ⓓ 0.5

47   Which number is a multiple of 12?

Ⓐ   3

Ⓑ   4

Ⓒ   36

Ⓓ   40

48   Miss Jenkins was packing 108 muffins into cardboard boxes. She placed 12 muffins in each cardboard box. Which equation can be used to find c, the number of cardboard boxes she used?

Ⓐ $c = 108 \div 12$

Ⓑ $c = 108 - 12$

Ⓒ $c = 108 \times 12$

Ⓓ $c = 108 + 12$

49 Rita made the pictograph below to show how many cans each grade 6 class collected for a food drive.

= 4 cans

How many cans did Mrs. Butler's class collect?

Write your answer on the line below.

_____

50 The table below shows the cost of hiring CDs, DVDs, and video games from a hire store.

Item	Cost per Week
CD	$2
DVD	$3
Video game	$4

Which expression represents the total cost of hiring c CDs and d DVDs for w weeks?

Ⓐ $2c + 3d + w$

Ⓑ $w(2c + 3d)$

Ⓒ $w(2c) + 3d$

Ⓓ $2c + 3d$

51   Sasha has 11 green blocks, 3 red blocks, 2 yellow blocks, and 4 blue blocks in a container. If she draws a block at random from the container, what is the probability that she will draw a yellow block?

(A) $\dfrac{1}{5}$

(B) $\dfrac{1}{10}$

(C) $\dfrac{1}{4}$

(D) $\dfrac{1}{8}$

52   The wingspan of the butterfly is 6.7 centimeters.

What is the wingspan of the butterfly in millimeters?

Write your answer on the line below.

_____

END OF TEST

STAAR MATH

GRADE 6

TEST 2

Instructions

The test contains multiple choice and open ended questions. Read each question carefully. For multiple choice questions, select the best answer and fill in the bubble for the answer you have chosen. For open ended questions, write your answer on the line.

You can use the mathematics charts on the next two pages to help you with some of the questions.

MATHEMATICS CHART

You may use this chart to help you answer questions in the test.

LENGTH

Metric	Customary
1 kilometer = 1000 meters	1 mile = 1760 yards
1 meter = 100 centimeters	1 mile = 5280 feet
1 centimeter = 10 millimeters	1 yard = 3 feet
	1 foot = 12 inches

CAPACITY AND VOLUME

Metric	Customary
1 liter = 1000 milliliters	1 gallon = 4 quarts
	1 gallon = 128 fluid ounces
	1 quart = 2 pints
	1 pint = 2 cups
	1 cup = 8 fluid ounces

MASS AND WEIGHT

Metric	Customary
1 kilogram = 1000 grams	1 ton = 2000 pounds
1 gram = 1000 milligrams	1 pound = 16 ounces

TIME

1 year = 365 days	1 day = 24 hours
1 year = 12 months	1 hour = 60 minutes
1 year = 52 weeks	1 minute = 60 seconds

MATHEMATICS CHART

You may use this chart to help you answer questions in the test.

Perimeter	square	$P = 4s$
	rectangle	$P = 2l + 2w$

Circumference	circle	$C = 2\pi r$ or $C = \pi d$

Area	square	$A = s^2$
	rectangle	$A = lw$ or $A = bh$
	triangle	$A = \frac{1}{2}bh$
	trapezoid	$A = \frac{1}{2}(b_1 + b_2)h$
	circle	$A = \pi r^2$

Volume	cube	$V = s^3$
	rectangular prism	$V = lwh$

Pi	π	$\pi \approx 3.14$

1 Glenn has 7 ties in his drawer. There are 5 plain ties and 2 patterned ties. If Glenn selects one tie without looking, what is the probability that he will select a plain tie?

Ⓐ 2 out of 7

Ⓑ 2 out of 5

Ⓒ 5 out of 7

Ⓓ 7 out of 10

2 Which of these is the best estimate of the length of a desk?

Ⓐ 4 inches

Ⓑ 4 feet

Ⓒ 4 yards

Ⓓ 4 miles

3   The table shows the amount of rainfall one week.

Day	Rainfall (cm)
Monday	4.59
Tuesday	4.18
Wednesday	4.5
Thursday	4.61
Friday	4.73

On which day was the rainfall the lowest?

Ⓐ   Monday

Ⓑ   Tuesday

Ⓒ   Thursday

Ⓓ   Friday

4   Ella competed in a running race. All the students finished the race in between 13.6 seconds and 14.4 seconds. Which of the following could have been Ella's time?

Ⓐ   13.05 seconds

Ⓑ   14.5 seconds

Ⓒ   14.49 seconds

Ⓓ   13.8 seconds

5   The table below shows a set of number pairs.

x	y
1	1
3	5
5	9

Which equation shows the relationship between *x* and *y*?

Ⓐ $y = 2x - 1$

Ⓑ $y = x + 2$

Ⓒ $y = x + 4$

Ⓓ $y = 2x$

6   Which number goes in the box to make the prime factorization of 168 correct?

$$2^{\square} \cdot 3 \cdot 7$$

Write your answer on the line below.

_____

7   Look at the fractions below.

$$1\frac{1}{3}, \ 2\frac{1}{2}, \ 3\frac{5}{6}$$

Which procedure can be used to find the sum of the fractions?

Ⓐ   Find the sum of the whole numbers, find the sum of the fractions, and then add the two sums

Ⓑ   Find the sum of the whole numbers, find the sum of the fractions, and then multiply the two sums

Ⓒ   Find the sum of the whole numbers, find the sum of the fractions, and then subtract the two sums

Ⓓ   Find the sum of the whole numbers, find the sum of the fractions, and then divide the two sums

8   The ratio of red roses to white roses in a bouquet was 3 to 2. If there were 12 red roses, how many white roses were there?

Write your answer on the line below.

_____

9   What kind of angle is angle Q?

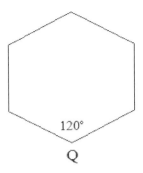

     ⒶacuteⒶ   Acute

     Ⓑ   Right

     Ⓒ   Obtuse

     Ⓓ   Straight

10   Chan's fish tank can hold 20 liters of water. How many milliliters of water can the fish tank hold?

     Ⓐ   200 mL

     Ⓑ   2 000 mL

     Ⓒ   20 000 mL

     Ⓓ   200 000 mL

11   Chloe is 61 inches tall, and is 2 inches taller than Craig. Craig is 3 inches taller than Callum. Which expression could be used to find Callum's height, in inches?

(A) $61 - 2 - 3$

(B) $61 + 2 + 3$

(C) $61 - 2 + 3$

(D) $61 + 2 - 3$

12   The four letter cards below were placed face down on a table. Aaron picks 2 letter cards.

Which list shows all the sets of two cards that Aaron could pick?

(A)   M and A, M and T, M and H

(B)   M and A, A and T, T and H

(C)   M and A, A and T, T and H, H and M

(D)   M and A, M and T, M and H, A and T, A and H, T and H

13 Byron made 9 baskets out of 14 baskets he attempted. About what percent of his baskets did he make?

Ⓐ   72%

Ⓑ   14%

Ⓒ   90%

Ⓓ   64%

14 William drew a quadrilateral on a coordinate grid, as shown below.

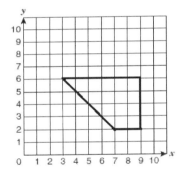

Which of these is NOT the coordinate of one of the vertices of the quadrilateral?

Ⓐ   (7, 2)

Ⓑ   (9, 2)

Ⓒ   (9, 6)

Ⓓ   (6, 3)

15 Which decimal is equivalent to the fraction $\frac{3}{8}$?

Ⓐ 0.125

Ⓑ 0.3

Ⓒ 0.375

Ⓓ 0.625

16 What is the perimeter of the triangle shown below?

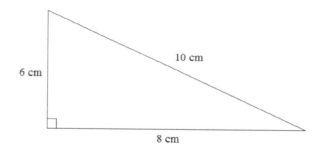

Ⓐ 12 cm

Ⓑ 22 cm

Ⓒ 24 cm

Ⓓ 48 cm

17 At a daycare center, there is 1 worker for every 5 children. There are 105 children at the daycare center. Which proportion can be used to find *x*, the number of workers?

Ⓐ $\dfrac{x}{5} = \dfrac{1}{105}$

Ⓑ $\dfrac{5}{1} = \dfrac{x}{105}$

Ⓒ $\dfrac{1}{5} = \dfrac{x}{105}$

Ⓓ $\dfrac{x}{1} = \dfrac{5}{100}$

18 Leanne added $\frac{1}{4}$ cup of milk and $\frac{3}{8}$ cup of water to a bowl. Which diagram is shaded to show how many cups of milk and water were in the bowl in all?

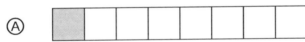

19 Brian made 16 paper cranes in 15 minutes. If he continues making cranes at this rate, how many cranes would he make in 2 hours?

Ⓐ   32

Ⓑ   64

Ⓒ   120

Ⓓ   128

20 A triangle is shown below.

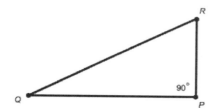

If angle *Q* measures 35°, what is the measure of angle *R*?

Ⓐ   35°

Ⓑ   55°

Ⓒ   75°

Ⓓ   145°

21 The cost of renting a windsurfer is a basic fee of $15 plus an additional $5 for each hour that the windsurfer is rented. Which equation can be used to find c, the cost in dollars of the rental for h hours?

Ⓐ $c = 15h + 5$

Ⓑ $c = 5h + 15$

Ⓒ $c = 15(h + 5)$

Ⓓ $c = 5(h + 15)$

22 The top of a side table has a diameter of 8 inches. What is the circumference of the top of the side table?

Ⓐ 4π inches

Ⓑ 8π inches

Ⓒ 16π inches

Ⓓ 64π inches

23   What is the measure of the angle shown below?

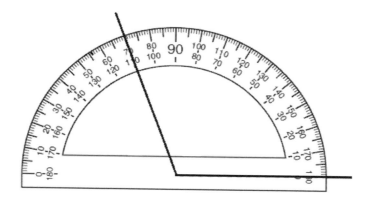

    Ⓐ   20°

    Ⓑ   70°

    Ⓒ   110°

    Ⓓ   120°

24   What is the greatest common factor of 6, 9, and 15?

Write your answer on the line below.

_____

25   The drawing below shows a quadrilateral.

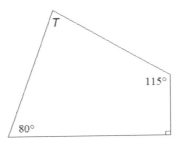

What is the measure of angle *T*, in degrees?

Write your answer on the line below.

_____

26   A pattern of numbers is shown below.

8, 13, 18, 23, 28, 33, 38, ...

If *n* is a number in the pattern, which rule can be used to find the next number in the pattern?

Ⓐ $n + 8$

Ⓑ $n - 8$

Ⓒ $n + 5$

Ⓓ $n - 5$

27   A class held a vote on where to go for a field trip. The results are shown below.

Location	Number of Votes
Museum	10
Cinema	5
Zoo	20
Town Hall	5

Chen decides to make a circle graph to show the results. Which section would make up a quarter of the graph?

Ⓐ   Museum

Ⓑ   Cinema

Ⓒ   Zoo

Ⓓ   Town Hall

28 Alice was placing pieces of cake on serving trays. She placed 6 pieces of cake on each serving tray. She filled a total of 18 serving trays. Which equation can be used to find c, the number of pieces of cake Alice used?

Ⓐ $c = 18 \div 6$

Ⓑ $c = 18 - 6$

Ⓒ $c = 18 \times 6$

Ⓓ $c = 18 + 6$

29 Greg's volleyball team returns 4 out of every 5 serves.

How many serves out of 100 would the team expect to return?

Ⓐ   45

Ⓑ   75

Ⓒ   80

Ⓓ   90

30 Which ordered pair represents a point located inside both triangles?

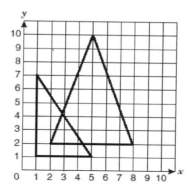

Ⓐ (2, 3)

Ⓑ (3, 3)

Ⓒ (4, 4)

Ⓓ (6, 1)

31 Which number is a multiple of 9?

Ⓐ 3

Ⓑ 20

Ⓒ 27

Ⓓ 35

32 Amy ordered 3 pizzas for $6.95 each. She also bought a soft drink for $1.95. Which equation can be used to find how much change she should receive from $30?

(A) $c = 30 - 3(6.95 + 1.95)$

(B) $c = 30 - 3(6.95 - 1.95)$

(C) $c = 30 - 6.95 - 1.95$

(D) $c = 30 - (6.95 \times 3) - 1.95$

33 Which of the following has a mass of about 1 gram?

(A) A dictionary

(B) A pen

(C) A car

(D) A paper clip

34 The table below shows how many customers a restaurant had on each day of the week.

Day	Number of Customers
Monday	28
Tuesday	21
Wednesday	36
Thursday	32
Friday	45

Which measure should be used to find the variation in the number of customers?

Ⓐ Mean

Ⓑ Median

Ⓒ Mode

Ⓓ Range

35 A restaurant has 120 customers and 6 waiters. What is the ratio of waiters to customers?

Ⓐ 1:6

Ⓑ 1:12

Ⓒ 1:20

Ⓓ 1:40

36 The drawing below shows a circle.

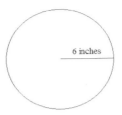

6 inches

What is the diameter of the circle?

Ⓐ   6π inches

Ⓑ   12 inches

Ⓒ   12π inches

Ⓓ   36π inches

37 Which of the following is most likely to have a mass of about 1 kilogram?

Ⓐ   A watermelon

Ⓑ   A grape

Ⓒ   An apple

Ⓓ   A banana

38   The table below shows how many students were in 7 dance classes.

Dance Class	Number of Students
Tap	18
Jazz	12
Ballet	10
Hip Hop	11
Jazz Ballet	10
Ballroom	14
Salsa	15

In which two dance classes were there a total of 30 students?

Ⓐ   Tap and Jazz

Ⓑ   Hip Hop and Ballroom

Ⓒ   Ballet and Jazz Ballet

Ⓓ   Ballroom and Salsa

39 Josephine wants to find the measure of an angle in a rhombus. Which tool should Josephine use?

    Ⓐ   Ruler

    Ⓑ   Protractor

    Ⓒ   Compass

    Ⓓ   Square

40 The table shows the side length of a rhombus and the perimeter of a rhombus.

Side Length, x (cm)	Perimeter, y (cm)
1	4
2	8
3	12
4	16

Which equation represents the relationship between side length and perimeter?

    Ⓐ $y = x + 3$

    Ⓑ $y = 4x$

    Ⓒ $x = y + 4$

    Ⓓ $x = 4y$

41   What is the mode of the following data?

14, 14, 17, 15, 18, 18, 14

Ⓐ   14

Ⓑ   18

Ⓒ   4

Ⓓ   15

42   A quadrilateral is shown below.

How many acute angles does the quadrilateral appear to have?

Ⓐ   0

Ⓑ   1

Ⓒ   2

Ⓓ   4

43 What is the least common multiple of 2, 3, and 6?

  (A) 6

  (B) 12

  (C) 18

  (D) 36

44 A picture frame has a length of 8 inches and a height of 6 inches.

What is the perimeter of the picture frame?

  (A) 28 inches

  (B) 36 inches

  (C) 42 inches

  (D) 48 inches

45 Samantha cut a piece of paper into pieces that were each $\frac{1}{5}$ the size of the original piece of paper. What decimal represents the size of each piece of paper compared to the original piece?

    Ⓐ   0.05

    Ⓑ   0.15

    Ⓒ   0.2

    Ⓓ   0.5

46 Which is the prime factorization of 198?

    Ⓐ $2 \cdot 3 \cdot 11$

    Ⓑ $2^2 \cdot 3 \cdot 11$

    Ⓒ $2^3 \cdot 3 \cdot 11$

    Ⓓ $2 \cdot 3^2 \cdot 11$

47   Maryann served part of a cake to her friends. The diagram below shows the amount of cake left.

What fraction of the cake is left?

Ⓐ $\dfrac{3}{8}$

Ⓑ $\dfrac{3}{4}$

Ⓒ $\dfrac{2}{2}$

Ⓓ $\dfrac{2}{6}$

48   The table below shows the total number of lemons in different numbers of bags of lemons.

Number of Bags	Number of Lemons
2	16
3	24
5	40
8	64

Which expression represents the number of lemons in x bags?

Ⓐ $2x$

Ⓑ $8x$

Ⓒ $16x$

Ⓓ $32x$

49 Keegan's family drinks about 2 gallons of milk every 5 days.

About how many gallons of milk does Keegan's family drink in 30 days?

Ⓐ   3 gallons

Ⓑ   6 gallons

Ⓒ   12 gallons

Ⓓ   30 gallons

50 A diner sells 3 sizes of sodas. The table shows the number of sodas of each size sold in 1 day.

Size	Amount
Small	162
Medium	257
Large	188

Which of these is the closest estimate of how many more medium sodas the diner sold than large sodas?

Ⓐ 70

Ⓑ 80

Ⓒ 90

Ⓓ 100

51 What is the value of the expression below?

$$42 + 24 \div 3 + 3$$

Ⓐ 22

Ⓑ 25

Ⓒ 46

Ⓓ 53

52   The table below shows the amount Davis spent on phone calls for four different months.

Month	Amount
April	$9.22
May	$9.09
June	$9.18
July	$9.05

Which month did Davis spend the most on phone calls?

Ⓐ   April

Ⓑ   May

Ⓒ   June

Ⓓ   July

END OF TEST

STAAR MATH

GRADE 6

TEST 3

Instructions

The test contains multiple choice and open ended questions. Read each question carefully. For multiple choice questions, select the best answer and fill in the bubble for the answer you have chosen. For open ended questions, write your answer on the line.

You can use the mathematics charts on the next two pages to help you with some of the questions.

MATHEMATICS CHART

You may use this chart to help you answer questions in the test.

LENGTH

Metric	Customary
1 kilometer = 1000 meters	1 mile = 1760 yards
1 meter = 100 centimeters	1 mile = 5280 feet
1 centimeter = 10 millimeters	1 yard = 3 feet
	1 foot = 12 inches

CAPACITY AND VOLUME

Metric	Customary
1 liter = 1000 milliliters	1 gallon = 4 quarts
	1 gallon = 128 fluid ounces
	1 quart = 2 pints
	1 pint = 2 cups
	1 cup = 8 fluid ounces

MASS AND WEIGHT

Metric	Customary
1 kilogram = 1000 grams	1 ton = 2000 pounds
1 gram = 1000 milligrams	1 pound = 16 ounces

TIME

1 year = 365 days	1 day = 24 hours
1 year = 12 months	1 hour = 60 minutes
1 year = 52 weeks	1 minute = 60 seconds

MATHEMATICS CHART

You may use this chart to help you answer questions in the test.

Perimeter	square	$P = 4s$
	rectangle	$P = 2l + 2w$

Circumference	circle	$C = 2\pi r$ or $C = \pi d$

Area	square	$A = s^2$
	rectangle	$A = lw$ or $A = bh$
	triangle	$A = \frac{1}{2}bh$
	trapezoid	$A = \frac{1}{2}(b_1 + b_2)h$
	circle	$A = \pi r^2$

Volume	cube	$V = s^3$
	rectangular prism	$V = lwh$

Pi	π	$\pi \approx 3.14$

1   Which of these units would be best to use to measure the mass of a laptop computer?

Ⓐ   Milligrams

Ⓑ   Kilograms

Ⓒ   Centimeters

Ⓓ   Meters

2   Brian checked in his bag at the airport. His bag weighed just over 21.9 kilograms. Which of the following could have been the weight of Brian's bag?

Ⓐ   20.9 kg

Ⓑ   21.4 kg

Ⓒ   22.1 kg

Ⓓ   20.0 kg

3 Look at the parallelogram below.

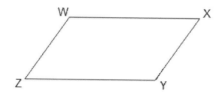

If the measure of angle Z is 40°, what is the measure of angle Y?

Ⓐ 40°

Ⓑ 50°

Ⓒ 140°

Ⓓ 280°

4 Lewis is making a scale drawing of his bedroom. He uses a scale of 1 inch equals 2 feet. The length of Lewis's bedroom is 12 feet. How would Lewis find how many inches long to draw his bedroom?

Ⓐ Divide 12 feet by 2 feet

Ⓑ Multiply 12 feet and 2 feet

Ⓒ Add 12 feet to 2 feet

Ⓓ Subtract 2 feet from 12 feet

5   The factor tree for the number 36 is shown below.

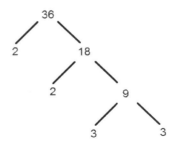

What is the prime factorization of 36?

Ⓐ $2^2 \cdot 3$

Ⓑ $2^2 \cdot 3^2$

Ⓒ $2 \cdot 3^2$

Ⓓ $2^2 \cdot 3^3$

6   On a trip to a shopping mall, it took Janelle 11 minutes to walk to the bus stop. She waited for the bus for 7 minutes, and was on the bus for 24 minutes. About how long did Janelle travel for in all?

Ⓐ   30 minutes

Ⓑ   40 minutes

Ⓒ   50 minutes

Ⓓ   60 minutes

7   The cost of renting a trailer is a basic fee of $20 plus an additional $25 for each day that the trailer is rented.

Which equation can be used to find c, the cost in dollars of the rental for d days?

Ⓐ $c = 20d + 25$

Ⓑ $c = 25d + 20$

Ⓒ $c = 20(d + 25)$

Ⓓ $c = 25(d + 20)$

8 The graph below shows the number of different types of trees in an orchard.

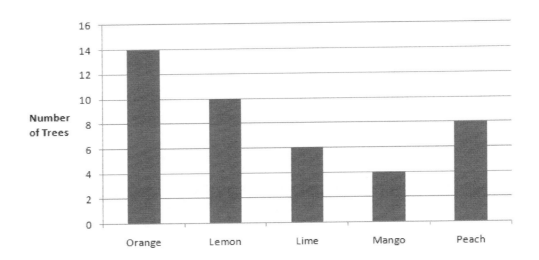

How many more orange trees are there than mango trees?

Ⓐ   10

Ⓑ   12

Ⓒ   14

Ⓓ   18

9   Brett records his best lap time each week he goes to swimming practice.

He wants to graph his best lap times to see how they have changed over the year. Which type of graph would Brett be best to use?

Ⓐ   Circle graph

Ⓑ   Line plot

Ⓒ   Line graph

Ⓓ   Stem and leaf plot

10   The ratio of apples to oranges in a fruit bowl was 2 to 5. If there were 10 apples, how many oranges were there?

Ⓐ   4

Ⓑ   20

Ⓒ   25

Ⓓ   50

11   What is the value of the expression below?

$$18 + 30 \div 2 - 1$$

Write your answer on the line below.

_____

12   The table below shows how many pages of a book Ryan read on 5 different days.

Day	Pages Read
Monday	20
Tuesday	30
Wednesday	15
Thursday	35
Friday	35

What is the median of the number of pages read?

Ⓐ   20

Ⓑ   27

Ⓒ   30

Ⓓ   35

13 Mrs. Williams is preparing lemonade for a birthday party. She wants each child to have exactly 2 cups of lemonade with no lemonade left over. She needs to use 4 lemons to make each cup of lemonade. How many lemons will she need to make enough lemonade for 12 children?

Ⓐ 6

Ⓑ 24

Ⓒ 48

Ⓓ 96

14 A sequence of numbers is shown below.

$$28, 24, 20, 16, 12, 8, 4, \ldots$$

Which procedure can be used to find the next number in the sequence?

Ⓐ Subtract 4 from the previous number

Ⓑ Add 4 to the previous number

Ⓒ Multiply the previous number by 2

Ⓓ Divide the previous number by 2

15   A quadrilateral is shown below.

How many obtuse angles does the quadrilateral appear to have?

Ⓐ   0

Ⓑ   1

Ⓒ   2

Ⓓ   4

16   A circle has a circumference of 5 inches. Which expression could be used to find the diameter of the circle?

Ⓐ $5 \div 2\pi$

Ⓑ $5 - 2\pi$

Ⓒ $5 \div \pi$

Ⓓ $5 + 2\pi$

17 Darrell sold drinks at a lemonade stand. The table shows how many drinks of each size he sold.

Size	Number Sold
Small	15
Medium	20
Large	5
Extra Large	10

What fraction of the drinks sold were medium drinks?

Ⓐ $\dfrac{1}{3}$

Ⓑ $\dfrac{2}{3}$

Ⓒ $\dfrac{2}{5}$

Ⓓ $\dfrac{1}{5}$

18 Mike went on vacation to Ohio. When he left home, the odometer read 7,219.4 miles. When he returned home, the odometer read 8,192.6 miles. How many miles did Mike travel?

Write your answer on the line below.

_____

19 The table below shows the different types of DVDs Taylor has.

Type of DVD	Number of DVDs
Action	3
Comedy	7
Drama	4
Science fiction	1

If Taylor picks 1 DVD without looking, what is the probability that she will pick a drama?

Ⓐ $\frac{7}{15}$

Ⓑ $\frac{4}{15}$

Ⓒ $\frac{3}{12}$

Ⓓ $\frac{7}{8}$

20 Pia is ordering business cards. She has to choose one pattern and one finish. Her choices are shown below.

Pattern	Finish
Plain	Plain
Stripes	Glossy
Stars	

How many different combinations are possible?

(A) 3

(B) 5

(C) 6

(D) 9

21 Michael answered 75% of the questions on a quiz correctly. What fraction of the questions did Michael answer correctly?

(A) $\frac{1}{25}$

(B) $\frac{1}{4}$

(C) $\frac{2}{5}$

(D) $\frac{3}{4}$

22 The table below shows the total number of pounds of flour in different numbers of bags of flour.

Number of Bags	Number of Pounds
3	12
5	20
8	32
9	36

Which expression represents the number of pounds of flour in x bags?

Ⓐ 3x

Ⓑ 4x

Ⓒ 6x

Ⓓ 9x

23   The drawing below shows a circle.

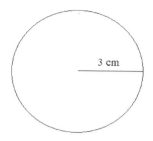

3 cm

Which expression can be used to find the circumference of the circle in centimeters?

Ⓐ   π x 3 x 2

Ⓑ $\frac{1}{2}$ x 3 x π

Ⓒ   π x 3

Ⓓ   π x 3^2

24   Jared is 128 centimeters tall. How tall is Jared in meters?

Ⓐ   0.128 m

Ⓑ   1.28 m

Ⓒ   12.8 m

Ⓓ   128 m

25 What is the measure of the angle shown below?

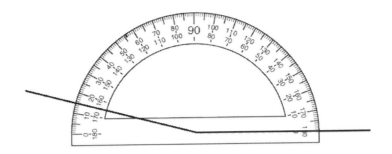

Ⓐ   15°

Ⓑ   25°

Ⓒ   165°

Ⓓ   175°

26 Which is the prime factorization of 256?

Ⓐ 2^6

Ⓑ 2^7

Ⓒ 2^8

Ⓓ 2^9

27 Triangle *XYZ* is an isosceles triangle. The measure of angle *X* is 22°. What is the measure of angle *Z*?

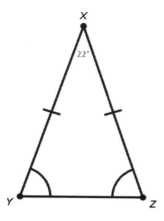

- Ⓐ 38°
- Ⓑ 79°
- Ⓒ 136°
- Ⓓ 158°

28 Kathy answered $\frac{3}{5}$ of the questions on a test correctly. Which of the following is equivalent to $\frac{3}{5}$?

- Ⓐ 30%
- Ⓑ 35%
- Ⓒ 60%
- Ⓓ 66%

29 The table below shows how long Chelsea spent doing yoga during the week.

Day	Time (minutes)
Monday	20
Tuesday	30
Wednesday	15
Thursday	35
Friday	35

What is the mean of the amount of time Chelsea spent doing yoga each day?

Ⓐ 20 minutes

Ⓑ 27 minutes

Ⓒ 30 minutes

Ⓓ 35 minutes

30 Which number is a multiple of 15?

Ⓐ 3

Ⓑ 5

Ⓒ 25

Ⓓ 45

31   Curtis made the graph below to show the locations of prizes he hid for a treasure hunt. Each star represents a treasure.

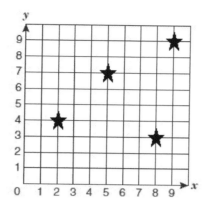

Which ordered pair represents a point where treasure can be found?

Ⓐ   (4, 2)

Ⓑ   (5, 6)

Ⓒ   (8, 4)

Ⓓ   (9, 9)

32   What kind of angle is angle S?

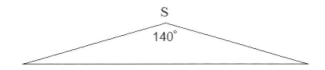

   Ⓐ   Acute

   Ⓑ   Right

   Ⓒ   Obtuse

   Ⓓ   Straight

33   Simon found that the air temperature inside was 17°C. After turning a heater on for an hour, the air temperature was 22°C. Which of these represents the change in temperature?

   Ⓐ   +5°C

   Ⓑ   −5°C

   Ⓒ   +7°C

   Ⓓ   −7°C

34 What is the rule to find the value of a term in the sequence below?

Position, n	Value of Term
1	2
2	5
3	8
4	11

Ⓐ $2n$

Ⓑ $n + 3$

Ⓒ $3n - 1$

Ⓓ $2n + 4$

35 Four screws have widths of $\frac{1}{2}$ inch, $\frac{1}{4}$ inch, $\frac{3}{4}$ inch, and $\frac{5}{8}$ inch. Which list shows these widths in order from greatest to least?

Ⓐ $\frac{1}{2}$ in, $\frac{1}{4}$ in, $\frac{3}{4}$ in, $\frac{5}{8}$ in

Ⓑ $\frac{3}{4}$ in, $\frac{5}{8}$ in, $\frac{1}{2}$ in, $\frac{1}{4}$ in

Ⓒ $\frac{1}{4}$ in, $\frac{1}{2}$ in, $\frac{5}{8}$ in, $\frac{3}{4}$ in

Ⓓ $\frac{5}{8}$ in, $\frac{3}{4}$ in, $\frac{1}{4}$ in, $\frac{1}{2}$ in

36 The grid below represents Casey's living room.

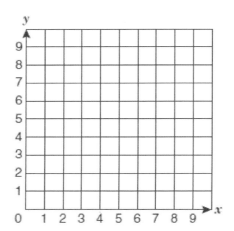

The television is located at the point (4, 4). A lamp is sitting 1 unit to the right of the television and 3 units up from the television. Which ordered pair represents the location of the lamp?

Ⓐ (3, 1)

Ⓑ (3, 7)

Ⓒ (5, 1)

Ⓓ (5, 7)

37 There are 128 people on a ship that has 16 lifeboats. What is the ratio of people to lifeboats?

Ⓐ   1:8

Ⓑ   1:16

Ⓒ   8:1

Ⓓ   16:1

38 What is the best estimate of the mass of a lemon?

Ⓐ   2 ounces

Ⓑ   2 pounds

Ⓒ   2 ton

Ⓓ   2 kilograms

39 Frankie swims laps of her pool each morning. It takes her 1.25 minutes to swim one lap. Which method can be used to find how many minutes it would take Frankie to swim 15 laps?

Ⓐ   Add 15 and 1.25

Ⓑ   Subtract 1.25 from 15

Ⓒ   Multiply 1.25 by 15

Ⓓ   Divide 15 by 1.25

40 During a golf game, Gia scored below par on 3 of the 18 holes.

How many holes would Gia be expected to score below par on if she played a total of 54 holes?

Ⓐ   6

Ⓑ   9

Ⓒ   12

Ⓓ   15

41   The table below shows the number of households in three different suburbs.

Suburb	Number of Households
Wellington	135,682
Ashton	179,441
Ellis	120,597

Which is the best estimate of the total number of households in the three suburbs, to the nearest ten thousand?

Ⓐ   400,000

Ⓑ   435,720

Ⓒ   436,000

Ⓓ   440,000

42 The table below shows the prices of items at a cake stall.

Item	Price
Small cake	$1.85
Muffin	$2.25
Cookie	$0.95

Frankie bought a small cake and a cookie. Bronwyn bought a muffin. How much more did Frankie spend than Bronwyn?

Write your answer on the line below.

_____

43 What is the greatest common factor of 15, 30, and 40?

Ⓐ   3

Ⓑ   5

Ⓒ   10

Ⓓ   15

44 Which diagram represents the sum of $\frac{1}{2}$ and $\frac{1}{8}$?

Ⓐ

Ⓑ

Ⓒ

Ⓓ

45 Raymond has a bag containing 5 red, 7 blue, 6 yellow, and 2 green marbles. If he randomly chooses one marble from the bag, what is the probability that the marble will be red?

Ⓐ $\frac{5}{6}$

Ⓑ $\frac{1}{3}$

Ⓒ $\frac{1}{4}$

Ⓓ $\frac{1}{6}$

46 The table shows the side length of an equilateral triangle and the perimeter of an equilateral triangle.

Side Length, *l* (inches)	Perimeter, *P* (inches)
2	6
3	9
4	12
5	15

Which equation represents the relationship between side length and perimeter?

Ⓐ $P = l + 4$

Ⓑ $P = 3l$

Ⓒ $l = P + 4$

Ⓓ $l = 3P$

47 What is the least common multiple of 4, 9, and 8?

    Ⓐ   288

    Ⓑ   36

    Ⓒ   32

    Ⓓ   72

48 Which figure below has the most obtuse angles?

    Ⓐ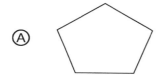

    Ⓑ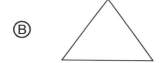

    Ⓒ

    Ⓓ

49 A pumpkin weighs 3.5 pounds. How many ounces does the pumpkin weigh?

Write your answer on the line below.

_____

50 Stacey is buying corn. She has $8 to spend. Corn is on sale for $2 per tray. Which additional information is needed to find the number of corn cobs that Stacey can buy?

Ⓐ The original price of the corn

Ⓑ The length of each corn cob

Ⓒ The number of corn cobs on a tray

Ⓓ The weight of each corn cob

51 The ratio of cars to motorbikes in a parking lot is 9 to 2. Which of these could be the number of cars and motorbikes in the parking lot?

Ⓐ 45 cars and 10 motorbikes

Ⓑ 90 cars and 40 motorbikes

Ⓒ 54 cars and 18 motorbikes

Ⓓ 72 cars and 8 motorbikes

52   Kenneth is making treat bags for a party. He has 80 balloons, 60 lollipops, and 30 toys. What is the greatest common factor Kenneth can use to divide the treats into equal groups?

ⓐ   2

ⓑ   5

ⓒ   10

ⓓ   20

END OF TEST

ANSWER KEY

Tracking Student Progress

Use the answer key to score each practice test. After scoring each test, record the score in the Score Tracker at the back of the book.

As the student progresses, test scores will continue to improve as the student gains experience, knowledge, and confidence.

Topics and Math Skills

The STAAR test given by the state of Texas tests a specific set of skills and knowledge. The skills and knowledge tested are divided into 5 broad objectives, or topics. These are:

- Numbers & Operations
- Patterns and Algebra
- Measurement
- Geometry
- Probability & Statistics

The answer key identifies the topic for each question. Use the topics listed to identify general areas of strength and weakness. Then target revision and instruction accordingly.

The answer key also identifies the specific math skill that each question is testing. Use the skills listed to identify skills that the student is lacking. Then target revision and instruction accordingly.

TEST 1 ANSWER KEY

Question	Answer	Topic	Math Skill
1	D	Probability & Statistics	Understand and interpret line plots
2	C	Geometry	Understand the angle measures of triangles
3	C	Measurement	Estimate measurements
4	C	Numbers & Operations	Use estimation
5	D	Patterns & Algebra	Use ratios to solve problems
6	C	Geometry	Identify and plot points on a coordinate grid
7	B	Geometry	Understand radius, diameter, and circumference
8	A	Patterns & Algebra	Represent ratios as fractions
9	D	Numbers & Operations	Use division to solve problems
10	B	Probability & Statistics	Calculate the mean of a data set
11	D	Numbers & Operations	Use estimation
12	A	Measurement	Measure angles
13	C	Measurement	Select appropriate measurement units
14	A	Patterns & Algebra	Use equations to represent situations
15	C	Numbers & Operations	Add fractions
16	C	Patterns & Algebra	Represent and describe sequences
17	A	Patterns & Algebra	Represent ratios as fractions
18	A	Geometry	Classify angles
19	34	Numbers & Operations	Use order of operations
20	B	Numbers & Operations	Identify common factors
21	C	Patterns & Algebra	Use ratios to solve problems
22	D	Probability & Statistics	Construct circle graphs
23	A	Geometry	Understand radius, diameter, and circumference
24	D	Numbers & Operations	Convert a fraction to a decimal
25	C	Geometry	Understand the angle measures of quadrilaterals
26	B	Measurement	Convert units of measure
27	D	Numbers & Operations	Compare and order decimals
28	A	Patterns & Algebra	Understand and write ratios
29	A	Geometry	Classify angles
30	A	Probability & Statistics	Calculate the mode of a data set
31	B	Probability & Statistics	Calculate the probability of a simple event
32	24	Numbers & Operations	Identify the least common multiple of a number set
33	A	Probability & Statistics	Select appropriate graphs
34	C	Numbers & Operations	Use integers to represent situations
35	B	Geometry	Identify and plot points on a coordinate grid
36	D	Numbers & Operations	Compare and order fractions
37	D	Geometry	Classify angles
38	A	Numbers & Operations	Add and subtract decimals
39	C	Numbers & Operations	Write prime factorizations
40	B	Patterns & Algebra	Use equations to represent situations
41	C	Patterns & Algebra	Use tables to generate formulas
42	C	Numbers & Operations	Identify the greatest common factor of a number set
43	B	Numbers & Operations	Model the addition of fractions

44	D	Measurement	Understand and calculate area
45	D	Probability & Statistics	Construct sample spaces for events
46	C	Numbers & Operations	Convert a fraction to a decimal
47	C	Numbers & Operations	Identify multiples of a number
48	A	Numbers & Operations	Use division to solve problems
49	32	Probability & Statistics	Understand and interpret pictographs
50	B	Patterns & Algebra	Use expressions to represent situations
51	B	Probability & Statistics	Calculate the probability of a simple event
52	67	Measurement	Convert units of measure

TEST 2 ANSWER KEY

Question	Answer	Topic	Math Skill
1	C	Probability & Statistics	Calculate the probability of a simple event
2	B	Measurement	Estimate measurements
3	B	Numbers & Operations	Compare and order decimals
4	D	Numbers & Operations	Compare and order decimals
5	A	Patterns & Algebra	Use equations to represent situations
6	3	Numbers & Operations	Write prime factorizations
7	A	Numbers & Operations	Understand how to add fractions
8	8	Patterns & Algebra	Use ratios to solve problems
9	C	Geometry	Classify angles
10	C	Measurement	Convert units of measure
11	A	Numbers & Operations	Use integers to represent situations
12	D	Probability & Statistics	Construct sample spaces for events
13	D	Patterns & Algebra	Represent ratios as percentages
14	D	Geometry	Identify and plot points on a coordinate grid
15	C	Numbers & Operations	Convert fractions to decimals
16	C	Measurement	Understand and calculate perimeter
17	C	Patterns & Algebra	Use ratios to describe proportional situations
18	C	Numbers & Operations	Model the addition of fractions
19	D	Patterns & Algebra	Use ratios to solve problems
20	B	Geometry	Understand the angle measures of triangles
21	B	Patterns & Algebra	Use equations to represent situations
22	B	Geometry	Understand radius, diameter, and circumference
23	C	Measurement	Measure angles
24	3	Numbers & Operations	Identify the greatest common factor of a number set
25	75	Geometry	Understand the angle measures of quadrilaterals
26	C	Patterns & Algebra	Represent and describe sequences
27	A	Probability & Statistics	Construct circle graphs
28	C	Numbers & Operations	Use multiplication to solve problems
29	C	Patterns & Algebra	Use ratios to solve problems
30	B	Geometry	Identify and plot points on a coordinate grid
31	C	Numbers & Operations	Identify multiples of a number
32	D	Numbers & Operations	Solve problems involving decimals
33	D	Measurement	Estimate measurements
34	D	Probability & Statistics	Understand range, mean, mode, and median
35	C	Patterns & Algebra	Understand and write ratios
36	C	Geometry	Understand radius, diameter, and circumference
37	A	Measurement	Estimate measurements
38	A	Numbers & Operations	Use integers to solve problems
39	B	Measurement	Select appropriate measurement tools
40	B	Patterns & Algebra	Use tables to generate formulas
41	A	Probability & Statistics	Find the mode of a data set
42	B	Geometry	Classify angles
43	B	Numbers & Operations	Identify the least common multiple of a number set

44	A	Measurement	Understand and calculate perimeter
45	C	Numbers & Operations	Convert fractions to decimals
46	D	Numbers & Operations	Write prime factorizations
47	B	Numbers & Operations	Model the addition of fractions
48	B	Patterns & Algebra	Use expressions to represent situations
49	C	Numbers & Operations	Use multiplication to solve problems
50	A	Numbers & Operations	Use estimation
51	D	Numbers & Operations	Use order of operations
52	A	Numbers & Operations	Compare and order decimals

TEST 3 ANSWER KEY

Question	Answer	Topic	Math Skill
1	B	Measurement	Select appropriate measurement units
2	C	Numbers & Operations	Compare and order decimals
3	C	Geometry	Understand the angle measures of quadrilaterals
4	A	Patterns & Algebra	Use ratios to solve problems
5	B	Numbers & Operations	Write prime factorizations
6	B	Numbers & Operations	Use estimation
7	B	Patterns & Algebra	Use equations to represent situations
8	A	Probability & Statistics	Understand and interpret bar graphs
9	C	Probability & Statistics	Select appropriate graphs
10	C	Patterns & Algebra	Use ratios to solve problems
11	32	Numbers & Operations	Use order of operations
12	C	Probability & Statistics	Calculate the median of a data set
13	D	Numbers & Operations	Use multiplication to solve problems
14	A	Patterns & Algebra	Represent and describe sequences
15	B	Geometry	Classify angles
16	C	Geometry	Understand radius, diameter, and circumference
17	C	Patterns & Algebra	Represent ratios as fractions
18	973.2	Numbers & Operations	Add and subtract decimals
19	B	Probability & Statistics	Calculate the probability of a simple event
20	C	Probability & Statistics	Construct sample spaces for events
21	D	Numbers & Operations	Convert a percentage to a fraction
22	B	Patterns & Algebra	Use expressions to represent situations
23	A	Geometry	Understand radius, diameter, and circumference
24	B	Measurement	Convert units of measure
25	C	Measurement	Measure angles
26	C	Numbers & Operations	Write prime factorizations
27	B	Geometry	Understand the angle measures of triangles
28	C	Numbers & Operations	Convert fractions to percentages
29	B	Probability & Statistics	Calculate the mean of a data set
30	D	Numbers & Operations	Identify multiples of a number
31	D	Geometry	Identify and plot points on a coordinate grid
32	C	Geometry	Classify angles
33	A	Numbers & Operations	Use integers to represent situations
34	C	Patterns & Algebra	Use expressions to represent sequences
35	B	Numbers & Operations	Compare and order fractions
36	D	Geometry	Identify and plot points on a coordinate grid
37	C	Patterns & Algebra	Understand and write ratios
38	A	Measurement	Estimate measurements
39	C	Numbers & Operations	Use multiplication to solve problems
40	B	Patterns & Algebra	Use ratios to solve problems
41	D	Numbers & Operations	Use estimation
42	$0.55	Numbers & Operations	Add and subtract decimals
43	B	Numbers & Operations	Identify the greatest common factor of a number set

44	C	Numbers & Operations	Model the addition of fractions
45	C	Probability & Statistics	Calculate the probability of a simple event
46	B	Patterns & Algebra	Use tables to generate formulas
47	D	Numbers & Operations	Identify the least common multiple of a number set
48	A	Geometry	Classify angles
49	56	Measurement	Convert units of measure
50	C	Numbers & Operations	Identify missing information
51	A	Patterns & Algebra	Use ratios to solve problems
52	C	Numbers & Operations	Identify the greatest common factor of a number set

ANSWER SHEET - TEST 1

1	Ⓐ Ⓑ Ⓒ Ⓓ	19	_____	37	Ⓐ Ⓑ Ⓒ Ⓓ
2	Ⓐ Ⓑ Ⓒ Ⓓ	20	Ⓐ Ⓑ Ⓒ Ⓓ	38	Ⓐ Ⓑ Ⓒ Ⓓ
3	Ⓐ Ⓑ Ⓒ Ⓓ	21	Ⓐ Ⓑ Ⓒ Ⓓ	39	Ⓐ Ⓑ Ⓒ Ⓓ
4	Ⓐ Ⓑ Ⓒ Ⓓ	22	Ⓐ Ⓑ Ⓒ Ⓓ	40	Ⓐ Ⓑ Ⓒ Ⓓ
5	Ⓐ Ⓑ Ⓒ Ⓓ	23	Ⓐ Ⓑ Ⓒ Ⓓ	41	Ⓐ Ⓑ Ⓒ Ⓓ
6	Ⓐ Ⓑ Ⓒ Ⓓ	24	Ⓐ Ⓑ Ⓒ Ⓓ	42	Ⓐ Ⓑ Ⓒ Ⓓ
7	Ⓐ Ⓑ Ⓒ Ⓓ	25	Ⓐ Ⓑ Ⓒ Ⓓ	43	Ⓐ Ⓑ Ⓒ Ⓓ
8	Ⓐ Ⓑ Ⓒ Ⓓ	26	Ⓐ Ⓑ Ⓒ Ⓓ	44	Ⓐ Ⓑ Ⓒ Ⓓ
9	Ⓐ Ⓑ Ⓒ Ⓓ	27	Ⓐ Ⓑ Ⓒ Ⓓ	45	Ⓐ Ⓑ Ⓒ Ⓓ
10	Ⓐ Ⓑ Ⓒ Ⓓ	28	Ⓐ Ⓑ Ⓒ Ⓓ	46	Ⓐ Ⓑ Ⓒ Ⓓ
11	Ⓐ Ⓑ Ⓒ Ⓓ	29	Ⓐ Ⓑ Ⓒ Ⓓ	47	Ⓐ Ⓑ Ⓒ Ⓓ
12	Ⓐ Ⓑ Ⓒ Ⓓ	30	Ⓐ Ⓑ Ⓒ Ⓓ	48	Ⓐ Ⓑ Ⓒ Ⓓ
13	Ⓐ Ⓑ Ⓒ Ⓓ	31	Ⓐ Ⓑ Ⓒ Ⓓ	49	_____
14	Ⓐ Ⓑ Ⓒ Ⓓ	32	_____	50	Ⓐ Ⓑ Ⓒ Ⓓ
15	Ⓐ Ⓑ Ⓒ Ⓓ	33	Ⓐ Ⓑ Ⓒ Ⓓ	51	Ⓐ Ⓑ Ⓒ Ⓓ
16	Ⓐ Ⓑ Ⓒ Ⓓ	34	Ⓐ Ⓑ Ⓒ Ⓓ	52	_____
17	Ⓐ Ⓑ Ⓒ Ⓓ	35	Ⓐ Ⓑ Ⓒ Ⓓ		
18	Ⓐ Ⓑ Ⓒ Ⓓ	36	Ⓐ Ⓑ Ⓒ Ⓓ		

ANSWER SHEET - TEST 2

#		#		#	
1	Ⓐ Ⓑ Ⓒ Ⓓ	19	Ⓐ Ⓑ Ⓒ Ⓓ	37	Ⓐ Ⓑ Ⓒ Ⓓ
2	Ⓐ Ⓑ Ⓒ Ⓓ	20	Ⓐ Ⓑ Ⓒ Ⓓ	38	Ⓐ Ⓑ Ⓒ Ⓓ
3	Ⓐ Ⓑ Ⓒ Ⓓ	21	Ⓐ Ⓑ Ⓒ Ⓓ	39	Ⓐ Ⓑ Ⓒ Ⓓ
4	Ⓐ Ⓑ Ⓒ Ⓓ	22	Ⓐ Ⓑ Ⓒ Ⓓ	40	Ⓐ Ⓑ Ⓒ Ⓓ
5	Ⓐ Ⓑ Ⓒ Ⓓ	23	Ⓐ Ⓑ Ⓒ Ⓓ	41	Ⓐ Ⓑ Ⓒ Ⓓ
6	_____	24	_____	42	Ⓐ Ⓑ Ⓒ Ⓓ
7	Ⓐ Ⓑ Ⓒ Ⓓ	25	_____	43	Ⓐ Ⓑ Ⓒ Ⓓ
8	_____	26	Ⓐ Ⓑ Ⓒ Ⓓ	44	Ⓐ Ⓑ Ⓒ Ⓓ
9	Ⓐ Ⓑ Ⓒ Ⓓ	27	Ⓐ Ⓑ Ⓒ Ⓓ	45	Ⓐ Ⓑ Ⓒ Ⓓ
10	Ⓐ Ⓑ Ⓒ Ⓓ	28	Ⓐ Ⓑ Ⓒ Ⓓ	46	Ⓐ Ⓑ Ⓒ Ⓓ
11	Ⓐ Ⓑ Ⓒ Ⓓ	29	Ⓐ Ⓑ Ⓒ Ⓓ	47	Ⓐ Ⓑ Ⓒ Ⓓ
12	Ⓐ Ⓑ Ⓒ Ⓓ	30	Ⓐ Ⓑ Ⓒ Ⓓ	48	Ⓐ Ⓑ Ⓒ Ⓓ
13	Ⓐ Ⓑ Ⓒ Ⓓ	31	Ⓐ Ⓑ Ⓒ Ⓓ	49	Ⓐ Ⓑ Ⓒ Ⓓ
14	Ⓐ Ⓑ Ⓒ Ⓓ	32	Ⓐ Ⓑ Ⓒ Ⓓ	50	Ⓐ Ⓑ Ⓒ Ⓓ
15	Ⓐ Ⓑ Ⓒ Ⓓ	33	Ⓐ Ⓑ Ⓒ Ⓓ	51	Ⓐ Ⓑ Ⓒ Ⓓ
16	Ⓐ Ⓑ Ⓒ Ⓓ	34	Ⓐ Ⓑ Ⓒ Ⓓ	52	Ⓐ Ⓑ Ⓒ Ⓓ
17	Ⓐ Ⓑ Ⓒ Ⓓ	35	Ⓐ Ⓑ Ⓒ Ⓓ		
18	Ⓐ Ⓑ Ⓒ Ⓓ	36	Ⓐ Ⓑ Ⓒ Ⓓ		

ANSWER SHEET - TEST 3

1	Ⓐ Ⓑ Ⓒ Ⓓ	19	_____	37	Ⓐ Ⓑ Ⓒ Ⓓ
2	Ⓐ Ⓑ Ⓒ Ⓓ	20	Ⓐ Ⓑ Ⓒ Ⓓ	38	Ⓐ Ⓑ Ⓒ Ⓓ
3	Ⓐ Ⓑ Ⓒ Ⓓ	21	Ⓐ Ⓑ Ⓒ Ⓓ	39	Ⓐ Ⓑ Ⓒ Ⓓ
4	Ⓐ Ⓑ Ⓒ Ⓓ	22	Ⓐ Ⓑ Ⓒ Ⓓ	40	Ⓐ Ⓑ Ⓒ Ⓓ
5	Ⓐ Ⓑ Ⓒ Ⓓ	23	Ⓐ Ⓑ Ⓒ Ⓓ	41	Ⓐ Ⓑ Ⓒ Ⓓ
6	Ⓐ Ⓑ Ⓒ Ⓓ	24	Ⓐ Ⓑ Ⓒ Ⓓ	42	_____
7	Ⓐ Ⓑ Ⓒ Ⓓ	25	Ⓐ Ⓑ Ⓒ Ⓓ	43	Ⓐ Ⓑ Ⓒ Ⓓ
8	Ⓐ Ⓑ Ⓒ Ⓓ	26	Ⓐ Ⓑ Ⓒ Ⓓ	44	Ⓐ Ⓑ Ⓒ Ⓓ
9	Ⓐ Ⓑ Ⓒ Ⓓ	27	Ⓐ Ⓑ Ⓒ Ⓓ	45	Ⓐ Ⓑ Ⓒ Ⓓ
10	Ⓐ Ⓑ Ⓒ Ⓓ	28	Ⓐ Ⓑ Ⓒ Ⓓ	46	Ⓐ Ⓑ Ⓒ Ⓓ
11	_____	29	Ⓐ Ⓑ Ⓒ Ⓓ	47	Ⓐ Ⓑ Ⓒ Ⓓ
12	Ⓐ Ⓑ Ⓒ Ⓓ	30	Ⓐ Ⓑ Ⓒ Ⓓ	48	Ⓐ Ⓑ Ⓒ Ⓓ
13	Ⓐ Ⓑ Ⓒ Ⓓ	31	Ⓐ Ⓑ Ⓒ Ⓓ	49	_____
14	Ⓐ Ⓑ Ⓒ Ⓓ	32	Ⓐ Ⓑ Ⓒ Ⓓ	50	Ⓐ Ⓑ Ⓒ Ⓓ
15	Ⓐ Ⓑ Ⓒ Ⓓ	33	Ⓐ Ⓑ Ⓒ Ⓓ	51	Ⓐ Ⓑ Ⓒ Ⓓ
16	Ⓐ Ⓑ Ⓒ Ⓓ	34	Ⓐ Ⓑ Ⓒ Ⓓ	52	Ⓐ Ⓑ Ⓒ Ⓓ
17	Ⓐ Ⓑ Ⓒ Ⓓ	35	Ⓐ Ⓑ Ⓒ Ⓓ		
18	Ⓐ Ⓑ Ⓒ Ⓓ	36	Ⓐ Ⓑ Ⓒ Ⓓ		

SCORE TRACKER

	Score
Test 1	/52
Test 2	/52
Test 3	/52

TEXAS TEST PREP STUDENT QUIZ BOOK

For additional test prep, get the Texas Test Prep Student Quiz Book. It contains one quiz for every skill tested on the Texas state test. It can be used in combination with this Practice Test Book for focused revision to target gaps in knowledge and address student weaknesses.

After revision using the quiz book, take another practice test and see the improvement!

TEXAS TEST PREP READING
Help with the Texas STAAR tests is also available for reading!

- Practice Test Book and Reading Workbook available
- Covers every reading skill needed by Texas students
  - Books available from Grades 3 through to 8

TEXAS TEST PREP MATH

Check out the full range of math books available!

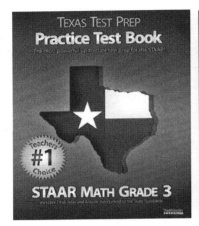 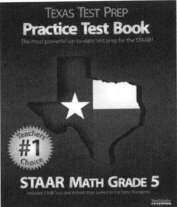 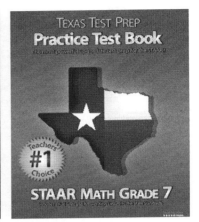

- Practice Test Book and Student Quiz Book available
- Covers every math skill needed by Texas students
- Books available from Grades 3 through to 8

 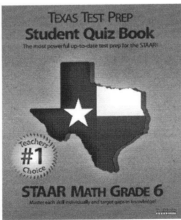 

22168641R00064

Made in the USA
Lexington, KY
15 April 2013